**COMBATING SPIRITUAL
STRONGHOLDS SERIES**

Over[c]

Fear

by
Rick Joyner

MorningStar Publications
Division of MorningStar Fellowship Church

P.O. Box 19409, Charlotte, NC 28219-9409

Overcoming Fear

Table of Contents

Chapter One
The Battle for the Soul of Man 5

Chapter Two
Good and Bad Fear 21

Chapter Three
Idols and Fears 31

Chapter Four
The Ultimate Idol vs.
the Ultimate Freedom 39

Chapter Five
The Security of the Force 51

Chapter Six
Pride Comes Before the Fall 61

Chapter Seven
The Road to the Kingdom 67

Chapter Eight
Peace and Prophecy 71

Chapter Nine
Summary 73

"There is no
fear in love;
but perfect love
casts out fear"
(I John 4:18)

Chapter One

The Battle for the Soul of Man

In these last days the battle raging for the soul of man is intensifying dramatically. This battle is being fought in every individual, every church, every city, and every nation. If we do not understand this conflict we will be defeated. This booklet is to help illuminate and tear down one of the most powerful weapons that the enemy of our souls is using to keep man in bondage to his evil ways. That weapon is FEAR!

The devil uses fear to keep the world under his power just as the Lord uses faith to set men free. Faith will lead us to the Lord's domain, which is His kingdom. There we find the liberty that releases us to be who we were created to be. This battle between faith and fear that rages in every soul will determine whether we live a successful life or not. The course of our lives will be dictated by faith or fear. We will all have to choose which it will be. Then we will have to fight. This message is to strengthen your hands for this battle, and to impart a resolve to overcome every fear that seeks dominion in your life, replacing it with a faith that climbs irresistibly toward the fulfillment of your individual purpose.

Though the basic course of our life is dictated by our submission to either fear or faith, there are degrees to this. We are under the control of evil to the degree that fear is allowed to control our life. That is why we are told in Romans 14:23, "**...for whatever is not from faith is sin**" (NKJV). If fear controls us, then fear is our lord. To walk in obedience to the Lord requires us to walk in faith. As we are told in Hebrews 10:38-39:

> **Now the just shall live by faith; but if anyone draws back, My soul has no pleasure in him."**
>
> **But we are not of those who draw back to perdition, but of those who believe to the saving of the soul (NKJV).**

Therefore, it should be a basic goal in our life to grow in faith, and to resist the control that fear has over us. This is a process that requires the renewing of our minds, or the very thinking by which we perceive and understand ourselves and the world around us. We will be the one that determines whether faith in God will control our actions and beliefs, or fears.

We should note that faith in God is always singular, but there are a multitude of fears that seek dominion over us. There is simplicity to the faith walk that is liberating. Fear is much more complicated. One of the most basic fears that seeks control of us is the fear of man. Under this category a multitude of fears will be found such as the fear of rejection, the fear of failure, the fear of embarrassment or humiliation, and so on. This is why the more we grow in faith in God, the more peace, rest, and fulfillment we will have in our life.

It is also noteworthy that most of our failures, rejections, and even humiliations are actually the result of fear that we have in those areas controlling us. Fear causes us to do things that we would not have done if we were living by faith in that area. As someone once said, "Fear is faith for the things you don't want," and in this way fear actually causes the release of the things we fear.

It's interesting that even the beasts can discern fear and react to it. Most of us have witnessed how a person who has a fear of dogs seems to arouse a desire to attack them in even the most docile pets. Animals that are predatory can immediately sense fear, and it arouses in them the aggression to catch their prey. This is the very thing that the enemy of our souls does to us spiritually. Fear arouses demonic forces to swarm to the vulnerable. Likewise, faith repels them.

From Demons to World Rulers

There are levels of demonic forces that are assaulting the world. These range from demonic attacks on individuals, to principalities that seek dominion over regions or whole nations, to "world rulers" that seek dominion or influence over the entire earth. When the terrorist leader Osama bin Laden prophesied that America would fear from North to South and East to West, he was issuing a demonic prophecy that was a clear indication of the enemy's strategy against America. Because the enemy is always seeking to counter the work of God, we can know for sure that faith is about to be released in America from North to South, East to West. We are in fact very close to the greatest of the Great Awakenings to ever sweep over this land.

As the enemy steps up his assault across the world to dominate foreign policy with fear and terror, we can be assured that it is the greatest opportunity for faith to be released in every place the enemy attacks. Faith is much more powerful than fear, and faith will ultimately prevail.

Earthly governments must fight the war against terror on the level of natural weapons, but only the church can achieve the ultimate victory over this enemy. As we are told in Ephesians 6:12: **"For our struggle is not against flesh and blood, but against the rulers, against the powers, against the world forces of this darkness, against the spiritual forces of wickedness in the heavenly places."** This is not a war against flesh and blood, but a spiritual battle that must be fought with spiritual weapons if we are going to have a true and lasting victory.

In the levels of power and authority discussed in the scripture above, we see demons assault individuals to gain influence over them until they have complete control over their actions. This is called being "possessed" by demons. Lesser levels of control by them are usually referred to as demonic oppression. Christians are given authority over demons, and no Christian who has come to know the authority of our Lord Jesus Christ should have a fear of being possessed by demons. In fact, if a Christian is walking in even the smallest amount of faith, this releases God's authority causing all demons on earth to fear and flee from us. Recognizing, confronting, and casting out demons is normal, biblical Christianity.

The next level of evil authorities addressed in Scripture are called "principalities and powers." As stated, these are greater than demons, and they seek domain over regions or nations, not just individuals. Though every Christian has the authority to cast out demons, we do not cast out principalities and powers, but must "wrestle" with them to displace them. This level of warfare is addressed in other books I have written such as *Epic Battles of the Last Days, Mobilizing the Army of God,* and *A Prophetic Vision for the 21st Century.*

Then there is another, higher realm of evil that are called "world rulers." These do not just affect individuals or regions, but can dominate much of the earth for ages. This level of evil I address in my book *Shadows of Things to Come.* Above this level is the evil lord, Satan himself. Christians are called to fight evil on all the levels. However, we only have true spiritual authority to the degree that the King lives within us, or to the degree that we abide in Him. As we grow in authority, which is evidenced by our increased faith, we will be called to fight battles on higher levels.

Generally, only demons will possess individuals, and the battle that most Christians face is a personal battle with the evil that tries to gain entrance to their own life. As we are victorious on this level and are trusted with more spiritual authority, we may be called on to confront evil on a higher level, seeking the liberation of a region, or even a nation from the enemy's domain. As my friend Francis Frangipane likes to say, "With new levels come new devils."

Francis has written what many consider to be the greatest book ever on spiritual warfare, *The Three Battlegrounds.* In this classic message he explains how our battle against evil starts with the battle in our own minds. As we gain victory there we must then fight for victory of the church. Only when the church is victorious in a region will it displace the principalities over it. This book is a very practical step-by-step advance toward such victories.

If we are going to be given national or international spiritual authority we can count on attacks from principalities and powers. If we have been given authority that will have an impact on the whole earth, or may span our own time, we will have to face a world ruler at some point. Paul the apostle was such a man, which is why he had to face Caesar. Because of Caesar's scope of authority he was not being manipulated by a mere demon, but by a world ruler. Because Jesus is the highest authority in the kingdom, He had to be confronted by Satan himself and prevail.

There are watershed events that cause sweeping changes over the whole earth. If these events are evil you can count on a "world ruler" being behind them. We witnessed such an event on September 11, 2001. This was the beginning of another strategic assault of fear that was on the level of a world ruler. This did not just affect the United States, but the whole world was shaken that day. It is right that the civilized governments of the world have now made terrorism the world's foremost enemy because it is. However, this is a spiritual enemy that cannot be defeated by mere bombs and bullets. Christians must overcome the fears that dominate their own lives, and then the church must overcome the same. We must now rise to the place of faith and authority confronting the world ruler that is assaulting the whole world.

Understanding the Two Mandates

This is not to negate the righteousness of the war in which our earthly governments are now engaged. As we are told concerning them in Romans 13:1-4:

> **Let every person be in subjection to the governing authorities. For there is no authority except from God, and those which exist are established by God.**
>
> **Therefore he who resists authority has opposed the ordinance of God; and they who have opposed will receive condemnation upon themselves.**
>
> **For rulers are not a cause of fear for good behavior, but for evil. Do you want to have no fear of authority? Do what is good and you will have praise from the same;**
>
> **for it is a minister of God to you for good. But if you do what is evil, be afraid; for it does not bear**

the sword for nothing; for it is a minister of God, an avenger who brings wrath upon the one who practices evil.

As this scripture states, civil governments have a mandate from God to avenge evil and bring wrath on those who practice evil on the earth. For this reason civil governments have been given the sword, or military power. We should always pray for our governments and pray for their success in bringing the wrath of God on those who practice evil. Throughout the Bible we see that most of the time when the Lord fulfilled His Word by bringing judgment upon a nation or people, it was done by using the military power of other nations.

This is essential for keeping order to the degree that it is possible until the kingdom of God comes to restore righteousness and justice on the earth. Because fallen men exercise this authority, it will not be exercised perfectly until the King comes. However, it does at least restrain a complete meltdown of order and authority. Civil authority is ordained by God, but it is not the kingdom of God.

As Christians we have a different mandate. We are not here in this age to avenge evil, but in fact are required to love our enemies, and pray for them. Our warfare is not against people, but whatever has people in bondage.

The greatest victory of all would be the repentance and salvation of our enemies. Many Christians have a difficult time understanding the two different mandates given to civil governments and to the church. However, this is something important that we must settle in our hearts if we are going to be effective in our job of tearing down the spiritual strongholds which keep men in bondage.

Our civil governments are fighting a righteous war against evil as they combat terrorism or governments that promote terrorism, but the church is called to a much different battle. We are called to fight the unseen war that is being waged in the heavenly places. Ours is a spiritual war.

This does not mean that Christians cannot join the military forces of nations to fight the war on the human level. However, they should understand that while marching under the orders of civil governments, their authority will be exercised through their physical weapons, not their spiritual ones. Nor does this mean that Christian soldiers should not pray, but if they are under orders from their civil government they must not hesitate to use the weapons that their government has given to them for fighting.

Likewise, if we are operating under the mandate given to the church we do not have authority to use weapons that are of the flesh for our battle. This is why "Christian militias" that arm themselves with guns or other physical weapons will always be motivated by fear and paranoia. They are actually controlled by evil since they are not properly under either of the mandates of authority that God has given to men.

Fight the Good Fight

Spiritual authority is something that we grow into. We are given more authority as we mature spiritually and are given higher commissions by the Lord. This will be evidenced by an increase of faith to new levels. We see in the book of Acts that Paul the apostle was called as an apostle many years before he was actually commissioned to that ministry. With that commissioning came authority on a higher level. However, **"…many are called, but few are chosen" (Matthew 22:14).** This means that many are called but few go on to receive their commission.

Being called to a high position does not give one authority. Maturity and the faithfulness that goes on to possess the promises is what will release true authority in us. However, we must understand that spiritual authority is not just given so we might have more respect from people, but so we can fight effectively against the powers that are destroying people.

As we are told in I John 3:8, "... **For this purpose the Son of God was manifested, that He might destroy the works of the devil**" (NKJV). As He prayed in John 17:18, just as He was sent into the world He has sent us, which means that we too are here to destroy the works of the devil. We have been given divinely powerful weapons for that purpose. We should all have notches in our belts for the enemy strongholds that we have brought down.

This book is intended to help us confront and overcome our personal demons and our personal fears, so that we can grow in the authority that will displace the evil from our families, churches, cities, nations, and ultimately the world. Because there is a faith that overcomes the world nothing less than this can be our goal. We may not see evil fully displaced until the King Himself returns to the earth, but there is a biblical mandate for us to do all we can to prepare the way for His coming kingdom by overcoming evil now. If we get carried away with too much faith and tear down some strongholds of evil that we were not called to tear down, I'm sure He will forgive us!

One of the ways the enemy has kept much of Evangelical, Pentecostal, and Charismatic Christianity in bondage has been to impart a belief that since it is inevitable the entire world is going to fall to the anti-Christ, it is useless to fight the evil in the world, therefore we should just try to be faithful ourselves and wait for the rapture. There are a number of Scriptures that challenge this deception, but let's just look at Daniel 11:31-32:

> **"And forces shall be mustered by him, and they shall defile the sanctuary fortress; then they shall take away the daily sacrifices, and place there the abomination of desolation.**

> **"Those who do wickedly against the covenant he shall corrupt with flattery; but the people who know their God shall be strong, and carry out great exploits (NKJV).**

Here we see that the very time the **"abomination of desolation"** is being set up, those who **"know their God"** are displaying strength and taking action! No one who really knows the Lord is going to just sit back and let evil take over.

Summary

The primary inroad that the enemy has into our lives, our families, our schools, and our world is through fear. We must take a stand against the fear that the enemy is seeking to increase over the whole world to enhance his control. We must determine right now that we will not let fear dictate the course of our lives, or our present actions. We are at war with fear.

As President Roosevelt said, "We have nothing to fear but fear itself." We can win this war. All we have to do is grow in faith. But true faith is not an ambiguous confidence in ourselves—it is the result of a living relationship with the God who loves us, has called us, and will empower us to do all that He created us to do.

The Lord Jesus said that the end of the age is the harvest (see Matthew 13:39). It is true that at the end of the age we are experiencing the greatest ingathering of souls into the kingdom in history. However, the harvest is also the time when everything that has been sown in man will come to full maturity, both the good and the evil. This is why we see in such Scriptures as Isaiah 60:1-5 the light and glory rising upon the Lord's people at the very time when **"darkness"** and even **"deep darkness"** will cover the people. Therefore, at the end of this age we can expect to see the ultimate yoke of bondage—fear, coming to its full maturity at the same time the Lord's people are experiencing the greatest levels of faith and peace.

We are about to experience the greatest fear and the greatest faith ever released on the earth. These will be taking place at the same time. If we are not growing in faith and the peace of God, we will be growing in fear and the anxiety that will ultimately even cause men's hearts to fail. Therefore, the ultimate answer to combating fear is to be growing in faith and the peace of God that goes beyond understanding.

We must first illuminate the evil nature of fear, and how it is used to place a multitude of shackles on our life. This illumination alone will begin to break that fear off of our lives. The enemy dwells in darkness, and whenever the light exposes him it quickly begins unraveling his power. Then we want to replace every fear in our life with a biblical, step-by-step strategy for growing in the faith, love, and peace of God.

Chapter Two
Good and Bad Fear

There is a good fear. The fear of God is good. **"The fear of the Lord is the beginning of wisdom"** (NKJV) as we are told in Psalm 111:10, Proverbs 9:10, and Job 28:28. When the pure and holy fear of the Lord reigns in our life we will not have to fear anything else. Our goal is to have only one fear in our life that is so great that it casts out all other fears.

To wake up those who are sleeping usually requires an alarm. An alarm is also a kind of fear, but it is good if it wakes us up. Even so, after being awakened we do not want to be controlled by the alarm, but by sound wisdom that is based on the fear of the Lord, which is actually a profound trust in the Lord.

The fact that the fear of the Lord is actually a kind of trust in Him seems to be a paradox. Such paradoxes in Scripture are often the places where the greatest treasures of wisdom and knowledge are found. Consider that we are told that jealousy is a work of the flesh in Galatians 5, and yet we are also told that God is a jealous God. Is God therefore subject to a work of the flesh by being jealous? Of course not. God's jealousy is not like man's, for it is not based on selfishness but on concern for us, and a devotion to truth. Neither is the fear of the Lord the same kind of fear that the devil is trying to darken the world with.

We need to establish that biblical paradoxes are not contradictions, but rather a view of something from different perspectives. There are also some apparent paradoxes that are created by the inadequacy of our language. These can usually be overcome with a little more effort, or just a little expansion of our biblical vocabulary.

The fear of the Lord is the beginning of wisdom, but it is not the ultimate end or the ultimate result of spiritual maturity. We begin with fear, but as we mature it turns to love, as we read in I John 4:16-19:

And we have known and believed the love that God has for us. God is love, and he who abides in love abides in God, and God in him.

Love has been perfected among us in this: that we may have boldness in the day of judgment; because as He is, so are we in this world.

There is no fear in love; but perfect love casts out fear, because fear involves torment. But he who fears has not been made perfect in love.

We love Him because He first loved us (NKJV).

Our goal should be to have the perfect love of God in our life that will cast out all evil fear. The fear of God is the beginning, or the foundation of wisdom. However, fear is not the highest wisdom—love is. Even so, a foundation is something that the whole building stands on. If it is not built correctly, the entire structure will be weak or even dangerous. If our understanding of the love of God is not first built on a solid foundation of the pure and holy fear of God, our understanding of His love will be perverted into a subtle form of man-centric humanism.

Lay a Good Foundation

To perceive the love of God is the higher wisdom. But those who jump straight to the higher floors of the building without laying a good foundation, will be building something that is quite shaky, and limits the greatness of what can ultimately be built. A primary weakness of modern, Western Christianity is the tendency of many believers to have a weak foundation of the fear of the Lord. Only when we have a strong foundation here will we be able to really comprehend the true love of God on the level that casts out all evil fear.

This is why the apostle Paul exhorts in Romans 11:22 to **"Behold then the kindness and the severity of God..."** Many who can see the kindness of God cannot see His severity—many who see His severity cannot see His kindness. However, if we are going to see Him as He is, we must be able to behold both His kindness and His severity together. These are not contradictory characteristics—He is kind in His severity, and severe in His kindness.

The Purity of Love

Even so, the bride of Christ is not going to purify herself to be without spot or wrinkle because she is afraid of what will happen if her Bridegroom finds her dress soiled. She is going to be without spot or wrinkle because she is so in love with Him that she wants to be perfect for Him, and puts forth the supreme effort to be that way. If you have ever been around a bride that is getting ready for her wedding you know the kind of focus and determination that she can have on this earth! This is what is going to come upon the bride of Christ, the church. Woe to anyone who gets in her way!

The bride of Christ began as a dirt-poor, filthy, little girl. When she first beheld the King in His glory, she was rightly appalled and fearful because of her condition. For her to be called into His great palace is an under-standably fearful thing. At first it is this awe and fear of the King that causes her to clean herself up to be near Him, but gradually she is so captured by His irresistible love that she will fall in love with Him. Then she will want to be pure and ready for Him because of her love. As her love grows so does this devotion.

To actually be called into the very family of God may be doctrinally understandable to a new believer, but in fact it is almost incomprehensible. To just be brought into the presence of the King is a fearful thought, as well it should be. He is God! But we will eventually overcome with His love. It is a part of the process of our minds being renewed that transforms us into an ever-deepening lover. However, as much as we grow in love we will never forget that He is God!

The Cross Is Love

If we do not go through this kind of process and transition, we will not realize how filthy we are, where we have come from, and how desperately we need the forgiveness of the cross. Or just as bad, we will not really comprehend His holiness. The deeper the realization of our sin, and the deeper the revelation of His holiness, the more we will be in the fear of the Lord for a time. This is right and necessary. This does not diminish just because we get cleaner, but because we realize more and more deeply His unconditional love.

However, to use this love as an excuse to continue in our sin is an ultimate affront to the cross and to His love. If we are touched by the true fear of the Lord and the true love of God, we will begin to hate sin just as He does. Sin does separate us from God, and after we come to truly know Him there is nothing more fearful than being separated from Him. Then, as we grow to love Him there is nothing more terrible than the pain that our sin causes Him.

We must also remember that when the Lord used the allegory comparing His church to being His bride, it was from the perspective of marriage in biblical times, not what it has become today in the West. In those times the King was the ultimate, absolute authority. Every man was the head of his household. Jesus is not calling us into some kind of loose partnership—it is an absolute commitment to His Lordship, as well as the most wonderful, intimate, and fulfilling relationship to the King of Glory.

The apostle John was the most intimate friend of the Lord's when He walked the earth. John then outlived all the other apostles so when he had the revelation on the Isle of Patmos he had known the Lord Jesus longer than anyone. Yet, as He beheld the glorified Lord Jesus whose breast he had once leaned against, he fell at His feet like a dead man!

Our God is truly an awesome God, and a much greater King than any king who has ever reigned on the earth! If we ever forget this we have fallen into a serious delusion.

Summary

The first step in the deliverance from fear is to have the right kind of fear—the fear of the Lord. That is why Solomon wrote in Proverbs 2:1-5:

> **My son, if you receive my words, and treasure my commands within you,**
>
> **So that you incline your ear to wisdom, and apply your heart to understanding;**
>
> **Yes, if you cry out for discernment, and lift up your voice for understanding,**
>
> **If you seek her as silver, and search for her as for hidden treasures;**
>
> **Then you will understand the fear of the LORD, and find the knowledge of God (NKJV).**

The fear of the Lord is a greater treasure than anything else we could possess on this earth. It is worth pursuing more than any earthly treasure. Now consider just a few of the great promises for those who have the fear of the Lord:

How great is Thy goodness, which Thou hast stored up for those who fear Thee, which Thou hast wrought for those who take refuge in Thee, before the sons of men! (Psalm 31:19)

Behold, the eye of the LORD is on those who fear Him, On those who hope for His lovingkindness,

To deliver their soul from death, and to keep them alive in famine (Psalm 33:18-19).

The angel of the LORD encamps around those who fear Him, and rescues them (Psalm 34:7).

O fear the LORD, you His saints; for to those who fear Him, there is no want.

The young lions do lack and suffer hunger; but they who seek the LORD shall not be in want of any good thing (Psalm 34:9-10).

For as high as the heavens are above the earth, so great is His lovingkindness toward those who fear Him (Psalm 103:11).

Just as a father has compassion on his children, so the LORD has compassion on those who fear Him (Psalm 103:13).

He will fulfill the desire of those who fear Him; He will also hear their cry and will save them (Psalm 145:19).

The LORD favors those who fear Him, those who wait for His loving-kindness (Psalm 147:11).

The fear of the LORD prolongs life, but the years of the wicked will be shortened (Proverbs 10:27).

In the fear of the LORD there is strong confidence, and his children will have refuge.

The fear of the LORD is a fountain of life, that one may avoid the snares of death (Proverbs 14:26-27).

The fear of the LORD leads to life, so that one may sleep satisfied, untouched by evil (Proverbs 19:23).

The reward of humility and the fear of the LORD are riches, honor and life (Proverbs 22:4).

Then those who feared the LORD spoke to one another, and the LORD gave attention and heard it, and a book of remembrance was written before Him for those who fear the LORD and who esteem His name.

"And they will be Mine," says the LORD of hosts, "on the day that I prepare My own possession, and I will spare them as a man spares his own son who serves him" (Malachi 3:16-17).

Chapter Three
Idols and Fears

The same power of God that was used to deliver Israel from her bondage destroyed the idols and power of Egypt. The power of God that becomes a sanctuary for His people will threaten all the other idols, works, and religions that keep His people in bondage. Why? Because the chains and many of our fears that keep us in bondage are linked to our idols. This is the result of allowing our bond to a thing to grow into bondage, and results in our developing irrational fears about losing them. It is for this purpose that we are given the exhortation in Hebrews 12:22-29:

> **But you have come to Mount Zion and to the city of the living God, the heavenly Jerusalem, to an innumerable company of angels,**
>
> **to the general assembly and church of the firstborn who are registered in heaven, to God the Judge of all, to the spirits of just men made perfect,**
>
> **to Jesus the Mediator of the new covenant, and to the blood of sprinkling that speaks better things than that of Abel.**

See that you do not refuse Him who speaks. For if they did not escape who refused Him who spoke on earth, much more shall we not escape if we turn away from Him who speaks from heaven,

whose voice then shook the earth; but now He has promised, saying, "Yet once more I shake not only the earth, but also heaven."

Now this, "Yet once more," indicates the removal of those things that are being shaken, as of things that are made, that the things which cannot be shaken may remain.

Therefore, since we are receiving a kingdom which cannot be shaken, let us have grace, by which we may serve God acceptably with reverence and godly fear.

For our God is a consuming fire (NKJV).

The point here is that a shaking is coming to the whole world, but we have a kingdom that **"cannot be shaken."** If we have built our lives on the kingdom that cannot be shaken, we will remain unshaken through whatever comes. If we have built our lives primarily on the kingdoms of this world, we will be shaken every time the world shakes. This was dramatically portrayed in the movie *The Ten Commandments*. One of the characters was a Hebrew who had so ingratiated himself to the Egyptians that they had elevated him to a position of prominence. Because of this he had more invested in Egypt than he did Israel, which caused the liberation of his Hebrew brothers and sisters to bring judgment upon him.

Where do we have the most invested? Where our treasure is there will our hearts be (see Matthew 6:21). Are our hearts more with this present world than in the kingdom? If so, we are going to be shaken when the earth shakes. The Lord is coming back to liberate the entire earth. When His kingdom comes, it will shake and bring down all of the kingdoms and idols that have been built on the fallen nature of man. We should only fear the shaking that is coming if we have built our lives more on the kingdoms of men than on the kingdom of God. Those who have rightly built their lives on the kingdom of God will not be shaken by what is coming, and neither will they fear it.

Not Even a Bump

I had a prophetic experience once in which I was suddenly standing in what appeared to be the radar room of a warship. I was standing in front of the radar screen, and the Lord was standing right next to me. Suddenly a blip appeared on the screen directly ahead and was coming closer. In such experiences you just know instinctively what to do, so I commanded that the ship turn 90 degrees to the right. The blip remained directly ahead and was still coming closer. I commanded the ship to be turned back to the left, but the blip remained directly ahead and coming right at us. I braced myself for the impact but nothing happened. I turned and asked the Lord what had just happened. He said that what I had seen on the radar screen was the time of great trouble or tribulation. He said that it was coming, and was unavoidable, but if I stayed close to Him I would not even feel it!

The Lord also spoke to me about our tendency to overemphasize the end of the age instead of preaching the coming of the kingdom. For too long we have allowed the enemy to take the high ground of hope for the future. There is no philosophy or religion on earth that has developed a concept of a utopia as great as the promise we have received for the age to come. I was told to stop living for the end of this age, and start living for the beginning of the age that is to come—the age in which He will reign over the earth in righteousness and justice. There will be such peace in His kingdom that the lion will lay down with the lamb, and children will be able to play with cobras, and no one will get hurt.

The Lord did not say that it was the gospel of salvation or the gospel of the church, but it is the gospel of the kingdom that must be preached before the end can come (see Matthew 24:14). To preach that gospel we must live in that kingdom. We declare it as ambassadors. Ambassadors are citizens whose true home is the country that they represent. Where is our true home?

This is not to imply that we cannot enjoy material things, but if we are going to be submitted to the kingdom of God and represent it, we must rule over things and not allow them to rule over us. Any wrong or excessive attachments that we have are an open door for the enemy, who will usually come through that door in the form of a fear.

Freedom

To represent the Lord and His kingdom without compromise we must be financially independent. This does not have to do with being wealthy or poor, but it means that we should never be in a place where our decisions are determined by financial considerations, but simply whether the matter is the will of God or not. We must be ruled by His kingdom, period. In His kingdom there are unlimited resources. However, these are not to be drawn on at our whim, but to do His will.

In Romans 1:5 and 16:26 Paul talks about the **"obedience to the faith."** True faith is directly linked to obedience. We obey the one we truly worship. An idol is not just something we worship, but it is anything we put our trust in that takes the place of God. For this reason we are warned in I Timothy 6:10-12:

> **For the love of money is the root of all evil: which while some coveted after, they have erred from the faith, and pierced themselves through with many sorrows.**
>
> **But thou, O man of God, flee these things; and follow after righteousness, godliness, faith, love, patience, meekness.**
>
> **Fight the good fight of faith, lay hold on eternal life, whereunto thou art also called, and hast professed a good profession before many witnesses (KJV).**

The love of money can be the root of all evil because it can be the ultimate idol that we put our trust in by allowing it to take God's rightful place. As this text declares, this always results in those who fall to it piercing themselves with many sorrows. This is because they fall to the bondage of many fears. This does not mean that we cannot be trusted with great wealth. The issue is do we have it, or does it have us?

If we have tasted the true wealth of the kingdom and beheld the true riches of God, having a lot of money, or a little, will not be of great concern to us. We just want enough to do His will. When we are in obedience to Him whose account we can never exhaust, we will not have either great fears or great desires for money or other forms of natural wealth. The more free we are in this area, the more we can then be trusted with.

The Lord needs people that He can trust with resources for the great work of His kingdom. The way His people handle money will be one of the distinguishing characteristics of the kingdom. Because the love of money can be one of the ultimate idols of the human heart, this will be one of the greatest tests at the end of the age.

Remember, the freedom of the kingdom is to walk in faith, and the bondage of this world is through fear. Our freedom from one of the ultimate yokes of bondage at the end of the age, the love of money, is to actually walk in the ultimate liberty that comes from being a slave of Christ. Understanding this paradox is one of the great truths that will set us free from one of the ultimate yokes of bondage.

Chapter Four

The Ultimate Idol vs. the Ultimate Freedom

Stewardship is the emphasis of a substantial portion of the Bible. Sound, biblical financial teaching must become an important emphasis for the church in our times. It is no accident that one of the ultimate tests at the end will be whether people will take the mark of the beast or not. This mark will be an economic mark. It will determine if we can buy, sell, or trade in this world. We will look at this in some detail in a moment, but first let us underscore some basic financial teachings in Scripture, always remembering that it is the truth that sets us free.

As the Lord made clear in the parable of the talents (see Matthew 25:14-30), we should seek to use everything the Lord has entrusted to us in the most profitable way. It is right that we give more emphasis to our spiritual gifts than our natural resources, but in this parable of the talents the Lord was talking about money. In biblical times "talents" were a form of currency. Recorded in Luke 16:10-13 we have another related exhortation from the Lord:

He who is faithful in a very little thing is faithful also in much; and he who is unrighteous in a very little thing is unrighteous also in much.

If therefore you have not been faithful in the use of unrighteous mammon, who will entrust the true riches to you?

And if you have not been faithful in the use of that which is another's, who will give you that which is your own?

No servant can serve two masters; for either he will hate the one, and love the other, or else he will hold to one, and despise the other. You cannot serve God and mammon.

That we cannot serve God and mammon means that we cannot combine the motive of serving God with the motive of making money. We must balance sound and wise financial management with keeping our primary motives, to that of seeking the purposes of the kingdom of God in everything we do. There is abundant evidence in our times that the love of money or poor financial management will corrupt ministry as well as individuals. This does not necessarily have anything to do with how much we have, since the poor can be more controlled by the love of money, or the desire for it, than the wealthy.

The Lord makes it clear in the previous text that we must learn to be faithful with worldly goods before we can be entrusted with the true riches of the kingdom. Learning to properly handle unrighteous mammon while maintaining a right spirit is important for every Christian. We see in the book of Revelation that one of the ultimate conflicts between the spirit of this world and the kingdom of God will revolve around economics, the ability to "buy, sell, and trade."

If prosperity is your primary goal, then you will serve the one who gives it to you. Just as Satan promised Jesus, if you will bow down to worship him, which is to live by his ways, then he will give you everything God has promised you. The devil will usually give it to you quickly—without having to go to the cross to get it. Jesus had already been promised all the kingdoms of the world. The temptation of Satan is to take the easy way, to attain the promise without going to the cross. Satan will promise you everything that God wants to give you, and he will also show you a quicker and easier way to attain them. Satan is the present ruler of this age and he can do it.

Taking the mark of the beast is not the sin that brings judgment—the sin is to worship the beast. The mark is simply evidence that one has been worshiping him. Will we escape judgment if we refuse to take a mark, but go on living our lives according to the ways of the beast? Of course not. Rather than being so concerned about the mark, we should be concerned about how we may be serving the beast or living according to his ways.

The mark of the beast is probably far more subtle than many have been led to believe, just as the mark of God is not literal, but spiritual. Even if it is a literal mark, the only way we will not take it is to already have the mark of God's bondservants. As we read in Revelation 7:1-3, this is the reason the events of these times have been restrained by the four angels who are holding back the winds. God is right now marking those who are true bondservants.

The Yoke of the Beast

The main reason Christians today are not free to respond to the call of God in their life is probably debt. When there is a call to do anything, from entering the ministry full-time to going on a mission trip, if our main consideration is whether or not we can afford it, then our financial condition rules us more than the will of God. It is also a revelation of just how much we have built our lives upon the foundations of this present age rather than on the kingdom of God, which is hearing and obeying the Word of the Lord.

Faith states that our situation can change. Regardless of how disobedient, or how foolish we have been, or how bad our situation is now, if we repent the Lord will deliver us. Our God really is all-powerful. When He helps there is no limit to what can be done. When His people are trapped with the hordes of the enemy bearing down on them, He delights in doing some of His greatest miracles. However, true faith begins with true repentance for whatever we have been doing that is wrong. Repentance does not just mean that we are sorry, but that we also turn away from our wicked ways.

As C.S. Lewis pointed out, in Christ, once we miss a turn and start down the wrong road, it will never become the right road. The only way we can get back on the right road is to go back to where we missed the turn. The Lord does not want to deliver us just to have us slip right back into bondage because we did not change our ways. Therefore, true repentance is evidence of the true faith that compels Him to respond.

Attaining Financial Independence

There is a clear biblical procedure for getting out and staying out of debt, and for becoming and remaining financially independent. The definition that I am using for financial independence is being in the place where you never have to make a decision based on financial considerations, but simply on the revealed will of God. This is the condition in which every Christian should live. This should be our first and most important financial goal. Regardless of how bad our present financial condition is, there is a very simple biblical formula that will provide a sure way of escape:

REPENTANCE + OBEDIENCE = FREEDOM

We must start by recognizing and repenting of any ways in which we have departed from the clear mandates of Scripture. Then we must begin to obey the clear and simple biblical instructions for financial management. If we do, we will escape our present situation and begin to live a life of freedom that is better than we have ever dreamed.

Wrong Thinking

Most of us think that the way out of our situation is to make more money. That is almost never the answer to financial problems, and can even make matters worse. God's plan for financial independence does not require us to make more money, and He is probably not going to give us a revelation so that we can win the lottery. We may not think there is any other way, but there is. If God can multiply the bread and the fish, He can make whatever we are now earning go just as far as He wants it to. All that we must do is obey the simple and clear instructions that He gave us in the Scriptures for managing what He entrusts to us.

Summary and Review

Because **"the love of money is the root of all evil," (I Timothy 6:10)** money tests some of the ultimate issues of the human heart. Idolatry is one of the ultimate offenses against God, and money is one of the primary idols in the world today. An idol was not just something that people feared or worshiped, but what they put their trust in. Money in itself is not evil, but how we relate to it can be a factor that determines the entire course of our life for good or evil.

Many sincere Christians still have idolatry in their hearts in relation to money, because they put more trust in their jobs or bank accounts than they do the Lord. Because we know that one of the ultimate tests that comes upon people living in the last days revolves around the "mark of the beast," which is an economic mark that determines whether we can buy, sell, or trade under his system, it is imperative that we confront this in our lives now.

In Revelation 7:1-3 we see that four angels are sent to hold back the four winds of the earth until the bondslaves of God have been marked on their foreheads. Believers have spent a great amount of time trying to figure out how the mark of the beast will come so they will not be fooled by it, but almost no attention to how we take the mark of God. The only way we will not take the mark of the beast is to have the mark of God. If God marks us we will never have to fear taking the enemy's mark.

The key to understanding the seal of God is understanding the bondservant—just as the key to understanding the mark of the beast is knowing that those who take the mark serve the beast.

Not all believers are bondservants. Many come to an understanding of the sacrifice of Jesus for their sins, but they still go on living their lives for themselves. We were the slaves of sin and the cross purchased us, so if we are Christ's we are no longer our own, we belong to Him. A bondservant does not live for himself, but for his master. This commitment is not just an intellectual agreement with certain biblical principles—it is the commitment to a radical lifestyle of obedience.

A bondservant does not have any money of his own, so he cannot spend freely what he has been entrusted with because it is not his. His time and even the family of a bond-servant belong to his master. To voluntarily become a slave is the ultimate commitment that can be made in this world. That is what it really means to embrace the cross. Those who are truly bondservants are the ones who will receive the Lord's mark.

Even though the Lord purchased us with His blood, He will not force anyone to be His bondservant. In Scripture a bondservant was one who was able to go free, but loved his master so much that he chose to be his slave for the rest of his life. We too, are free to choose whether we will be bondservants or not. God allows us to choose whether we will serve Him or not because freedom is required for true worship or true obedience from the heart. There can be no obedience from the heart unless there is the freedom to disobey.

We are free to go on living for ourselves, but it is the ultimate folly. We must know the Lord as our Source and keep our trust in Him. The key to our survival in this time is being a bondservant to the Lord. Every master is obligated to provide for his slaves, and we have the most dependable Master of all. He will take care of His own.

Being a bondservant of the Lord is to become His slave, but it is also the greatest freedom we can ever know in this life. When we are united with Him, by taking His yoke, we die to this world just as He did. When we are truly dead to the world there is nothing the world can do to us. It is impossible for a dead man to fear, to be offended, or to feel remorse because he loses some of his possessions. To the degree that we fear the loss of our possessions or positions, is the degree to which we are still not dead to these things. The enemy uses fear to bind us just as the Lord uses faith to set us free.

When we are dead to this world, but alive to Christ, we have Him, so all the treasures of this earth seem petty and insignificant. When we are seated with the King of kings on His throne, what pull can an earthly position have for us? This does not mean we do not have a genuine care for our jobs or ministries here, but we care for them because He has entrusted them to us, and we do them as worship unto Him. If our positions here are taken from us, we are still seated with Him, and we will worship Him in whatever way He calls us to next. We are His slaves, and we must be content with whatever job He gives to us.

When Christ is our life, our trust, and the true desire of our heart, He can then trust us with earthly possessions and positions that we are called to rule over. But if He is not our life, our trust, and the desire of our heart, our possessions and positions will inevitably rule over us. Whoever or whatever rules over us is in fact our lord. We are entering a time when the Lordship of Jesus must be more than a doctrine—it must be the profound and continuing reality in our life, then we will be free indeed. When we are fully yoked to Him, having cast off all the yokes of this present evil age, He will then be free to trust us with the unlimited resources of His kingdom.

Chapter Five
The Security of the Force

The very first thing that God said was not good was for man to be alone. This is quite interesting because when the Lord said this, man had God at the time. Wasn't God enough for man? As shocking as the answer may seem to some, the answer is "no." The Lord created men to need Him, but also to need other human beings. Man needed a wife and they both needed a family. Then they all needed the fellowship of the community.

Our relationship to God should be the most fulfilling part of our life, but it is not wrong for us to need fellowship with others too. Relationships are crucial in our life. The fear versus faith principle works in relationships too. Developing good social skills is crucial to developing and keeping good relationships. Having good social skills gives one a considerable amount of confidence in life, which dispels many fears that can otherwise have devastating control of us.

I remember well the confusion of my teenage years. Because of serious family problems mine were probably more confusing than most. I remember how astonished

I was at the peace that came into my life almost immediately upon entering the military. I was trained, equipped, and given a specific function in something that was much bigger than I was. I had a secure place, and could advance to the degree that my skills developed. Similarly, this is what the body of Christ is supposed to be to a world that is sinking into increasing social confusion.

The prophet Joel had a vision of a mighty army of God that was coming upon the earth. A force is about to be released like the world has never seen, which is described in Joel 2:1-11:

> **Blow a trumpet in Zion, and sound an alarm on My holy mountain! Let all the inhabitants of the land tremble, for the day of the LORD is coming; surely it is near,**
>
> **A day of darkness and gloom, a day of clouds and thick darkness. As the dawn is spread over the mountains, so there is a great and mighty people; there has never been anything like it, nor will there be again after it to the years of many generations.**
>
> **A fire consumes before them, and behind them a flame burns. The land is like the garden of Eden**

before them, but a desolate wilderness behind them, and nothing at all escapes them.

Their appearance is like the appearance of horses; and like war horses, so they run.

With a noise as of chariots they leap on the tops of the mountains, like the crackling of a flame of fire consuming the stubble, like a mighty people arranged for battle.

Before them the people are in anguish; all faces turn pale.

They run like mighty men; they climb the wall like soldiers; and they each march in line, nor do they deviate from their paths.

They do not crowd each other; they march everyone in his path. When they burst through the defenses, they do not break ranks.

They rush on the city, they run on the wall; they climb into the houses, they enter through the windows like a thief.

Before them the earth quakes, the heavens tremble, the sun and the moon grow dark, and the stars lose their brightness.

And the LORD utters His voice before His army; surely His camp is very great, for strong is he who carries out His word. The day of the LORD is indeed great and very awesome, and who can endure it?

There is a fire in the army of God that will destroy wood, hay, and stubble, but it will purify gold, silver, and precious stones. It will consume what man has built, and reveal what was indeed built by God. What is coming will be either terrible or glorious depending on what we have built our lives upon. The earth will literally quake at the presence of the Lord in the midst of this army that is now being mobilized. The Word of God that will be in their mouths will shatter the idols of this world like a hammer shattering rocks. The Spirit that is in them will be an irresistible force.

Finding our place in God's army, which is His church, is becoming increasingly critical. We cannot make it alone. As the breakdown of the social order of nations continues, the body of Christ will become a much more clearly defined, disciplined, and powerful social force in the earth. We will ultimately be as disciplined as the best army that ever marched. Every one will know their specific place in this army, and will all march in line, not crowding each other, but supporting one another in the great advance that is coming. Those who are in this army will know increasing peace and security. Those who are not in their place will be subject to increasing fear.

Choose Your Weapon

It is another paradox, but we cannot be a part of this great army until we are firmly established in the peace of God. One of the most powerful spiritual weapons that has been given to God's people is peace. We may think that peace is not a weapon, but it is such a weapon that Paul did not write that it was the Lord of hosts, or the Lord of armies, who would crush the enemy, but said **"the *God of peace* will soon crush Satan under your feet" (Romans 16:20).** When we abide in the peace of God it is both a fortress and a weapon that the enemy has no power against.

If we abide in the peace of God in a situation, it unravels the enemy's power over that situation. That is why most attacks of the enemy upon believers are intended to first rob them of their peace. The peace of God is the linchpin fruit of the Spirit that must be in place to hold all of the others in their place. Once we lose the peace of God we will quickly lose our patience, love, self-control, etc. This causes us to fall from our position of abiding in Christ, and the fruit of the Spirit will always demonstrate our abiding in Him.

Because we represent the Prince of Peace, and it is the peacemakers who are called the sons of God (see Matthew 5:9), it is the church that the world should be turning to for the solutions to its conflicts. Our victory over evil is accomplished by overcoming it with good. We destroy the enemy's power of destruction by standing in and imparting peace.

However, instead of the world turning to the church for solutions to its conflicts, the church is now viewed more as a source of conflicts. This will change. The church is called to judge the world, and as conflicts and anxiety grow in the world, peace and wisdom are going to grow in the church to such an extent that even the heathen will start coming to Christians for help. Through this the church's spiritual authority will grow stronger and stronger as lawlessness erodes human authority.

The church is the **"Jerusalem above,"** the spiritual Jerusalem that Paul mentions in Galatians 4:26. Jerusalem means "city of peace." Like the earthly Jerusalem, the church is now embroiled in almost continuous strife with war within herself as well as against the forces of the world without. Even so, she is going to soon be victorious over the strife within, and will then be able to turn all of her great weapons on the forces without.

The church will arise to fulfill her purpose in all that she is called to do and be. It will be as foretold in Isaiah 60:1-2, when darkness will increase, and deep darkness will come upon the people and the Lord's glory will rise and appear upon His people. When human conflict and strife reach unprecedented levels, the church will know unprecedented peace. This peace will be a fortress that will be impregnable to the enemy. Then the church will become the true sanctuary on earth.

Presently, just as there is no human solution to the conflict in the Middle East, there is no human solution to the conflict within the church. The solution is in God alone. The peace of God is rooted in knowing that God is God, and that Jesus is the King above all kings, rulers, and authorities. When we see that He is in control we come to understand deep in our hearts that Romans 8:28 is true, **"And we know that God causes all things to work together for good to those who love God, to those who are called according to His purpose."** When we know in our hearts that this is true there is no power on earth that can steal our peace.

When we abide in the peace of God regardless of what the circumstances are, it crushes Satan's attempts to use those circumstances, and it also allows us to see God's purpose in them. The Lord is not in heaven wringing His hands over a single problem on earth. He knows the end from the beginning, and He already knows what He is going to do to make things right. If we are abiding in Him, seated with Him in the heavenly places as we are called to do, we too will dwell in perfect peace. As we are promised in Isaiah 26:3, **"The steadfast of mind Thou wilt keep in perfect peace, because he trusts in Thee."** That is why Paul uttered the great prayer recorded in Ephesians 1:18-23:

> **I pray that the eyes of your heart may be enlightened, so that you may know what is the hope of His calling, what are the riches of the glory of His inheritance in the saints,**
>
> **and what is the surpassing greatness of His power toward us who believe. These are in accordance with the working of the strength of His might**
>
> **which He brought about in Christ, when He raised Him from the dead, and seated Him at His right hand in the heavenly places**
>
> **far above all rule and authority and power and dominion, and every name that is named, not only in this age, but also in the one to come.**

And He put all things in subjection under His feet, and gave Him as head over all things to the church,

which is His body, the fulness of Him who fills all in all.

The **"eyes of our heart"** are our spiritual eyes. When they are open, we will see Jesus where He sits, *far above* all authority, power, and dominion on the earth. As we begin to see Him there, and walk in His truth, living our lives in the unfathomable peace this brings, it crushes the influence of Satan in our life. This is what King David understood when he wrote Psalm 46:10-11, **"Cease striving and know that I am God; I will be exalted among the nations, I will be exalted in the earth. The LORD of hosts is with us; the God of Jacob is our stronghold."**

When we really know that He is God, we will cease striving. When His people come to this knowledge and walk in it, He will be **"exalted among the nations."** The peace of God will be in such profound contrast to the fears that are coming upon the world causing people's hearts to fail. Peace will be one of the greatest witnesses of the Lord in the midst of His people.

Chapter Six

Pride Comes Before the Fall

Pride caused the fall of Satan and almost every fall since. We know that "…**God is opposed to the proud, but gives grace to the humble"(James 4:6),** and we are told in I Peter 5:6-7, **"Humble yourselves, therefore, under the mighty hand of God, that He may exalt you at the proper time, casting all your anxiety upon Him, because He cares for you."** This implies that one of the ways we humble ourselves is to cast our anxiety upon the Lord. This is because anxiety is a form of pride that actually asserts that we think the matter is too big for God so we will have to handle it ourselves. If we really believe that He is God we will cease striving, and we will also cast off our anxiety and live in the peace that comes from knowing that He is in control.

It is no accident that "panic attacks" have now reached epidemic proportions. Anxiety is rising dramatically in the world, but peace will rise correspondingly in those who are true followers of Christ. The anxiety that is coming upon the world is the direct result of man trying to live without God and do everything on his own. That is why the original temptation of man was to get him to try to become what God had in fact called him to be, but to do it without God.

The more mankind turns from God, the more striving and confusion there will be, which will result in even more fear. This increases impatience, self-centeredness, and other "works of the flesh" that cause conflict. Christians must not live as the world lives. We must grow in the knowledge of the Lord's authority and control. We must grow in the peace of God.

Walking in Truth

If we are going to crush Satan under our feet we also need to understand that this metaphor "crush Satan under our feet" is used for a purpose. This speaks that his power is being broken through our "walk," our going forth. Christianity is not static, but is always moving forward, growing. That is why the River of Life is a river and not a pond or a lake. A river is always flowing, proceeding toward its destination.

When we walk in the peace of God in our home, it will ultimately crush the enemy's influence there. If we walk in the peace of God at work, it will soon crush the enemy's influence there. If the Christians in a city would walk in the peace of God, the church there would soon come into unity, and the enemy's influence over that city would be crushed. When Christians in any nation begin to truly walk in the peace of God, they will crush the enemy's influence over that nation.

God's Barometer

God's prophetic barometer of the condition of humanity is the nation of Israel. Almost everyone who visits Israel reports that it is one of the most intense places on earth. The citizens of Israel live under unceasing pressure and anxiety. It now seems that the nation of Israel will do almost anything for peace, even giving up precious land that they paid such a high price for in blood and hardship. However, no amount of change in the external conditions will bring Israel the peace that she seeks, but God has a remedy.

After years of inquiring of the Lord to know what we could do as a ministry for Israel, I was told to send "missionaries of peace" to live there. Their main calling is to walk in the peace and rest of God, so their joy and peace in the midst of the stress would stand out as an oasis in contrast to the spirit now prevailing over that nation. When the believers who live there are delivered of anxiety and begin to walk in the peace of God, it will be the most striking witness of the Prince of Peace that Israel has had since the first century. When this is demonstrated, it will make this peace of heart even more desirable than peace with the nations around them. There is no peace like the peace of God, and this alone can lead to a true peace among those neighbors.

The enemy has sent onslaught after onslaught to disturb Israel, but peace will be victorious. The true peace is the condition of heart that trusts God regardless of the circumstances. When this happens we are close to receiving the marching orders for the greatest army of God that will ever have been released upon the earth.

If we are going to understand the times we must heed the Lord's own exhortation in Mark 13:28-29, **"Now learn the parable from the fig tree: when its branch has already become tender, and puts forth its leaves, you know that summer is near. "Even so, you too, when you see these things happening, recognize that He is near, right at the door."** Because the fig tree is a symbol of Israel, this is an exhortation to understand this nation as a sign of the times. It is wisdom to be concerned about the events in Israel and seek to understand what they mean.

It is also noteworthy that when Agabus prophesied in the first century that a famine was coming upon the whole earth, the way the Christians prepared for it was to take up an offering for the believers in Israel. They understood God's promise to bless those who bless Abraham's seed. They also understood that God had established an eternal law in the beginning that a seed could only reproduce after its own kind. If we want to be blessed in the natural, bless the natural seed of Abraham. If we are seeking spiritual blessing, bless the spiritual seed of Abraham, which is the church. By blessing the natural seed which are the believers, we are blessing both together.

Chapter Seven
The Road to the Kingdom

Who are you now warring with? What is the source of the greatest conflict in your life? Have you cast this anxiety upon the Lord? When you do this exercise of faith, it will release Him to move into this situation. That is why we are told in Hebrews 12:14-15, **"Pursue peace with all men, and the sanctification without which no one will see the Lord. See to it that no one comes short of the grace of God; that no root of bitterness springing up causes trouble, and by it many be defiled."**

There is no reason for a Christian to ever be bitter at anyone or anything. If we are bitter we are being defiled, and we will also defile others with it. As Dudley Hall once said, "Bitterness is like drinking poison and hoping someone else gets sick." We are called to something much higher than this. We are called to the ultimate nobility of soul that is reflected in forgiveness, and the ultimate dignity that comes from walking in the peace of God.

Define the sources of conflict and agitation in your life and repent of your lack of faith and trust in the Lord in relation to them. Cast this anxiety upon the Lord, and determine that regardless of appearances or situations, you are going to trust the Lord to deal with the matters. He will do it, but usually after He has dealt with something even more important—your own heart.

The lack of peace in our lives is directly related to the lack of faith that we have in the Lord. A fundamental calling on our lives is simply to trust God. That is why the Lord said, **"...This is the work of God, that you believe in Him whom He has sent" (John 6:29).** Simply trusting Him everyday will accomplish much more than many of the works and projects that we try to do for Him. The church and the kingdom that Jesus is building are in our hearts, and will be manifested in our daily lives. The Lord does not judge the quality of a church by how good the meeting is Sunday morning, but by how good the people are on Monday morning.

The peace of God is the power that will lead us to victory over ourselves and the strongholds of the enemy. We are all called to be missionaries of the peace of God. This peace is not the result of peaceful conditions, but is a profound confidence in God even in the midst of the most trying conditions. The more stressful or violent the conditions, the more the peace of God is a demonstration of the true faith in God. This faith is what moves the Lord to take action on our behalf in those conditions. Peace is therefore an accurate barometer of the true level of our faith.

Our Fortress

How do we build our lives upon this kingdom that cannot be shaken? Romans 14:17 states, **"for the kingdom of God is not eating and drinking, but righteousness and peace and joy in the Holy Spirit."** Those who do not know God are always in an endless pursuit of joy and happiness, but it can never be attained outside of Christ. We will never know true peace without building our lives on a foundation of righteousness, which is simply having a right relationship with God.

When we are living lives that are obedient to the Lord and His ways, peace will be the result. With this peace, which comes from knowing that we are right with God, comes the true joy that is beyond anything that we can experience in the world. This is because man was created to have fellowship with God and nothing but intimacy with Him will ever satisfy the deepest longing of our soul.

Because the Lord made us and knows what we need, the righteousness of God is simply living the way we were created to live, doing that which is in fact the best for us. What is best for us is walking with God, dwelling in His presence, following the King, and being obedient to Him in all things. That is righteousness, and it brings peace that cannot be shaken and a joy that is eternal.

It is now time to be armed with the peace of God. Those who do, will go forth conquering in His name. The peace of God is an impregnable fortress. Never, ever, lose your peace, and you will always know victory.

In I Thessalonians 5:23 Paul prayed, **"Now may the *God of peace* Himself sanctify you entirely; and may your spirit and soul and body be preserved complete, without blame at the coming of our Lord Jesus Christ."** It is **"the God of peace"** who will sanctify us, for it is by abiding in the peace of God that we abide in the Lord. Sanctification is not just a state of not sinning, but it is abiding in the Lord. When we abide in Him, we will not just renounce sin, but we will love and we will have faith for the true works of God.

Chapter Eight
Peace and Prophecy

We are told in Philippians 4:7, **"And the peace of God, which surpasses all comprehension, shall guard your hearts and your minds in Christ Jesus."** It is interesting the Greek word that is translated "guard" in this text is *phroureo* (froo-reh'-o), comes from a compound word that means "to be a watcher in advance, i.e. to mount guard as a sentinel (post spics at gates); figuratively, to hem in, protect: or to keep as with a garrison." The peace of God not only keeps our hearts and minds in Christ, it helps us to see in advance, and to know what to do to protect against the attacks of the enemy.

This is one of the primary lessons that the church should have learned from those who got caught up in the Y2K scare. Every prophecy that I personally witnessed about the imminent doom that Y2K would bring had an air of anxiety and fear attached. As we read in James 3:17-18:

> **But the wisdom from above is first pure, then peaceable, gentle, reasonable, full of mercy and good fruits, unwavering, without hypocrisy.**

71

And the seed whose fruit is righteousness is sown in peace by those who make peace.

If the peace of God is going to guard our hearts and minds in Christ Jesus we must learn to not receive that which comes without the peace of God attached. I realize many people can hear a pure word from the Lord that is sown in peace and still be afraid. Before we can discern in this way, our own hearts must be at peace. Having the peace of God rule in our hearts, our families, and our churches must be a high priority if we are going to be free from deception.

Chapter Nine

Summary

The Scriptures are clear that difficult times are coming upon the world, but at the same time the glory of the Lord will be coming upon His people. Hearing the prophecies about difficulties should not disturb us, but they should awaken us, and help to prepare us. This will only be true as we abide in the peace of God, which keeps us abiding in God.

The Lord is not sitting in the heavens worrying about anything, and neither will those who are abiding in Him. If we are abiding in Him the whole world can collapse around us and we will be in perfect peace because we have built our lives on a kingdom that cannot be shaken.

When Jesus was tempted by the devil, He answered every temptation with Scripture. The Word of God is stronger than any power that we will ever be faced with. Now is the time to search the Scriptures, taking our stand on that which will stand forever—the Word of God. Consider the following promises of His peace. They are sure so that we should never be troubled. If we will abide in His peace, we will prevail against any fortress the evil one can build.

The LORD will give strength to His people; the LORD will bless His people with peace (Psalm 29:11).

If we are abiding in the Lord we will be abiding in His peace as well. If anxiety is growing in our life it is because we have somehow become separated from Him. If this has happened it is always on our part, not His. Therefore, we should ask the Holy Spirit to convict us of our sin, repent of what is revealed to us as the cause of the separation, and resolve to grow in both peace and faith. It is the Lord's will to bless you with His peace, and for you to abide in it. As we are told in Psalm 85:8-9:

> **I will hear what God the LORD will say; for He will speak peace to His people, to His godly ones; but let them not turn back to folly. Surely His salvation is near to those who fear Him, that glory may dwell in our land.**

Our dwelling place should be full of the glory of the Lord. If it is not, make finding out why the top priority in your life. I Peter 3:10-11 reveals a primary reason why many do not have peace in their lives, and are not walking in the glory:

> **For, let him who means to love life and see good days refrain his tongue from evil and his lips from speaking guile. And let him turn**

away from evil and do good; let
him seek peace and pursue it.

Are our words and actions sowing peace
and unity? Remember, we will all reap what
we are sowing. A primary reason why many,
and possibly most, are not walking in the
peace of God or experiencing His glory in
their life is because of what comes from their
own tongues. For this reason let us heed the
words of King David in Psalm 34:14: **"Depart
from evil, and do good; seek peace, and
pursue it."** As Peter wrote, **"Therefore,
beloved, since you look for these things,
be diligent to be found by Him in peace,
spotless and blameless" (II Peter 3:14).**

Why Did He Come?

Of course we know that Jesus came into
this world to redeem us, but it is by our
walking in His peace that we have evidence
of His salvation, as we read in Luke 1:76-79:

**And you, child, will be called
the prophet of the Most High; for
you will go on before the LORD to
prepare His ways;**

**to give to His people the
knowledge of salvation by the
forgiveness of their sins,**

**because of the tender mercy of
our God, with which the Sunrise
from on high shall visit us,**

to shine upon those who sit in darkness and the shadow of death, to guide our feet into the way of peace.

He came **"to guide our feet into the way of peace."** Are we following Him? If we are we should be growing in faith and peace, and experiencing less fear and anxiety. It is for this reason that Isaiah declares that the increase of His government will also result in an increase of peace.

For a child will be born to us, a son will be given to us; and the government will rest on His shoulders; and His name will be called Wonderful Counselor, Mighty God, Eternal Father, Prince of Peace.

There will be no end to the increase of His government or of peace..." (Isaiah 9:6-7).

Therefore, to the degree that the kingdom of God grows in us, we will also grow in peace. Please consider carefully these other promises concerning the peace of God. Each one is worth more than any treasure on this earth.

"Peace I leave with you; My peace I give to you; not as the world gives, do I give to you. Let not your heart be troubled, nor let it be fearful (John 14:27).

How lovely on the mountains are the feet of him who brings good

news, *who announces peace* and brings good news of happiness, who announces salvation, and says to Zion, "Your God reigns!" (Isaiah 52:7)

So shall My word be which goes forth from My mouth; it shall not return to Me empty, without accomplishing what I desire, and without succeeding in the matter for which I sent it.

For you will go out with joy, *and be led forth with peace*; the mountains and the hills will break forth into shouts of joy before you, and all the trees of the field will clap their hands (Isaiah 55:11-12).

Pray for the peace of Jerusalem: May they prosper who love you.

May peace be within your walls, and prosperity within your palaces.

For the sake of my brothers and my friends, I will now say, *"May peace be within you."*

For the sake of the house of the LORD our God I will seek your good (Psalm 122:6-9)

The LORD is my light and my salvation; whom shall I fear? The LORD is the defense of my life; whom shall I dread?

When evildoers came upon me to devour my flesh, my adversaries and my enemies, they stumbled and fell.

Though a host encamp against me, My heart will not fear; though war arise against me, in spite of this I shall be confident.

One thing I have asked from the LORD, that I shall seek: that I may dwell in the house of the LORD all the days of my life, to behold the beauty of the LORD, and to meditate in His temple.

For in the day of trouble He will conceal me in His tabernacle; in the secret place of His tent He will hide me; He will lift me up on a rock (Psalm 27:1-5).

Light arises in the darkness for the upright; He is gracious and compassionate and righteous.

It is well with the man who is gracious and lends; He will maintain his cause in judgment.

For he will never be shaken; the righteous will be remembered forever.

He will not fear evil tidings; His heart is steadfast, trusting in the LORD.

His heart is upheld, he will not fear, until he looks with satisfaction on his adversaries.

He has given freely to the poor; His righteousness endures forever; His horn will be exalted in honor (Psalm 112:4-9).

Do not be wise in your own eyes; fear the LORD and turn away from evil.

It will be healing to your body, and refreshment to your bones.

Honor the LORD from your wealth, and from the first of all your produce;

So your barns will be filled with plenty, and your vats will overflow with new wine.

My son, do not reject the discipline of the LORD, or loathe His reproof,

For whom the LORD loves He reproves, even as a father, the son in whom he delights.

How blessed is the man who finds wisdom, and the man who gains understanding.

For its profit is better than the profit of silver, and its gain than fine gold.

She is more precious than jewels; and nothing you desire compares with her.

Long life is in her right hand; in her left hand are riches and honor.

Her ways are pleasant ways, *and all her paths are peace*.

She is a tree of life to those who take hold of her, and happy are all who hold her fast.

The LORD by wisdom founded the earth; by understanding He established the heavens.

By His knowledge the deeps were broken up, and the skies drip with dew.

My son, let them not depart from your sight; keep sound wisdom and discretion,

So they will be life to your soul, and adornment to your neck.

Then you will walk in your way securely, and your foot will not stumble.

When you lie down, you will not be afraid; when you lie down, your sleep will be sweet.

Do not be afraid of sudden fear, nor of the onslaught of the wicked when it comes;

For the LORD will be your confidence, and will keep your foot from being caught.

Do not withhold good from those to whom it is due, when it is in your power to do it (Proverbs 3:7-27).